Nephi Runs Away

written by Tiffany Thomas
illustrated by Nikki Casassa

CFI · An imprint of Cedar Fort, Inc. · Springville, Utah

HARD WORDS:
Nephite, Lamanite, people

PARENT TIP: When your child is stuck on a word, do not say the word for them. Count to five in your head, and then share a strategy to figure it out. (Look at the picture, sound it out, etc.)

Nephi is Lehi's son.

Lehi dies.
Nephi is the new prophet.

Nephi's brother
Laman is mad.

Laman does not want to hear Nephi.

God tells Nephi
to run away.

Nephi and his family run away.

All the good people go with Nephi.

The bad people stay with Laman.

Nephi's people are called Nephites.

Laman's people are called Lamanites.

God keeps the Nephites safe.

The end.

ISBN 13: 978-1-4621-4337-5

Published by CFI, an imprint of Cedar Fort, Inc. • 2373 W. 700 S., Suite 100, Springville, UT 84663
Distributed by Cedar Fort, Inc., www.cedarfort.com

Cover design and interior layout design by Shawnda T. Craig
Cover design © 2022 Cedar Fort, Inc.
Printed in China • Printed on acid-free paper
10 9 8 7 6 5 4 3 2 1